The Ritual of the Pure Land Dakinis Requesting the Spiritual Guide to Remain

Heartfelt Requests for the Long Life of
Geshe Kelsang Gyatso Rinpoche

The Ritual of the Pure Land Dakinis Requesting the Spiritual Guide to Remain

Heartfelt Requests for the Long Life of
Geshe Kelsang Gyatso Rinpoche

Geshe Kelsang Gyatso Rinpoche

The Ritual of the Pure Land Dakinis Requesting the Spiritual Guide to Remain

After ceremoniously escorting the Guru (or a representation of him) into the Gompa and inviting him to sit on the throne, the disciples should first make three prostrations. Then begin Offering to the Spiritual Guide *in the usual manner, reciting it up to the end of the inner offering verse. At this point the tsog offering is made. At the end of the invocation prayer that precedes the actual tsog offering, the five Dakinis enter in the following sequence: blue, yellow, red, green, and white, and dance to the throne. They come before the throne, take up the scarf in their respective colour, and remain there while the tsog offering is made.*

After the Guru has tasted the tsog offering (AH HO MAHA SUKHA) the main part of Offering to the Spiritual Guide *is resumed with the secret offering verse. After the request for the Guru to turn the Wheel of Dharma, the actual* Ritual of the Pure Land Dakinis *begins with a request to the Dakinis to return to the Pure Land without the Guru.*

Requesting the Dakinis not to take the Spiritual Guide to the Pure Land

O Dakini of the Vajra family in the east,
With a blue-coloured body and a blue complexion,
Together with your retinue, a myriad of blue Dakinis,
To you hosts of blue Ladies I make this request:
Please accept this torma and tsog offering
And dissolve the eastern silk into the Dharmadhatu.
Please render assistance to all practitioners
And especially protect the life of our glorious Spiritual
Guide.

As the scarf is cut and the rice is thrown, the Dakini departs, receiving offerings as she leaves.

O Dakini of the Ratna family in the south,
With a yellow-coloured body and a yellow complexion,
Together with your retinue, a myriad of yellow Dakinis,
To you hosts of yellow Ladies I make this request:
Please accept this torma and tsog offering
And dissolve the southern silk into the Dharmadhatu.
Please render assistance to all practitioners
And especially protect the life of our glorious Spiritual
Guide.

As the scarf is cut and the rice is thrown, the Dakini departs, receiving offerings as she leaves.

O Dakini of the Päma family in the west,
With a red-coloured body and a red complexion,
Together with your retinue, a myriad of red Dakinis,
To you hosts of red Ladies I make this request:
Please accept this torma and tsog offering
And dissolve the western silk into the Dharmadhatu.
Please render assistance to all practitioners
And especially protect the life of our glorious Spiritual
Guide.

As the scarf is cut and the rice is thrown, the Dakini departs, receiving offerings as she leaves.

O Dakini of the Karma family in the north,
With a green-coloured body and a green complexion,
Together with your retinue, a myriad of green Dakinis,
To you hosts of green Ladies I make this request:
Please accept this torma and tsog offering
And dissolve the northern silk into the Dharmadhatu.
Please render assistance to all practitioners
And especially protect the life of our glorious Spiritual
    Guide.

As the scarf is cut and the rice is thrown, the Dakini departs, receiving offerings as she leaves.

O Dakini of the Buddha family in the centre,
With a white-coloured body and a white complexion,
Together with your retinue, a myriad of white Dakinis,
To you hosts of white Ladies I make this request:
Please accept this torma and tsog offering
And dissolve the central silk into the Dharmadhatu.
Please render assistance to all practitioners
And especially protect the life of our glorious Spiritual
    Guide.

As the scarf is cut and the rice is thrown, the Dakini departs, receiving offerings as she leaves.

Requesting the Spiritual Guide to remain

O Gurus, to you we make this request
For the blessings of the lineage of the Father and Sons.
May the stable, unchanging body of our glorious Guru,
Endowed with the majesty of the major and minor
    marks,
Remain on this seat of a lion throne, lotus, moon, and
    sun.

O Guru, remain unchanging on this vajra seat.
Please remain on this unchanging vajra seat.
O Lord of Buddha's doctrine please remain.
Please remain for the sake of migrating beings.
Please remain for the sake of beings as extensive as
    space.
Please remain until samsara has ceased.

O Gurus, to you we make this request
For the blessings of the lineage of the Father and Sons.
May the stable, unchanging speech of our glorious Guru,
Unceasingly proclaiming the sound of Dharma with a
    melodious voice,
Remain on this seat of a lion throne, lotus, moon, and
    sun.
O Guru, remain unchanging on this vajra seat.
Please remain on this unchanging vajra seat.
O Lord of Buddha's doctrine please remain.
Please remain for the sake of migrating beings.
Please remain for the sake of beings as extensive as
    space.
Please remain until samsara has ceased.

O Gurus, to you we make this request
For the blessings of the lineage of the Father and Sons.
May the stable, unchanging mind of our glorious Guru,
Endowed with compassion and all-knowing wisdom,
Remain on this seat of a lion throne, lotus, moon, and
    sun.
O Guru, remain unchanging on this vajra seat.
Please remain on this unchanging vajra seat.
O Lord of Buddha's doctrine please remain.
Please remain for the sake of migrating beings.
Please remain for the sake of beings as extensive as
    space.
Please remain until samsara has ceased.

Offering the vajra seat

The principal supplicant makes three prostrations and stands before the Guru holding the embroidered vajra.

This throne is a vajra throne pure from the beginning,
A vajra throne that is clear, empty, and unapprehendable,
A vajra throne that is the union of appearance and
    empty,
A throne of which there is no higher,
Considering this, please remain on this throne.

Now the vajra seat is offered:

This seat is a stainless lotus seat,
A sun seat that dispels the darkness of ignorance,
A moon seat that is the nature of clear light,
A seat of which there is no higher,
Considering this, please remain on this seat.

This assembly is a vast assembly of Sangha,
An assembly of Heroes manifesting their deeds,
An assembly of Heroines fulfilling the supreme
    purpose,
An assembly of which there is no higher,
Considering this, please remain within this assembly.

This land is a completely Pure Land of the Conquerors,
A land where the venerable Buddhas of the three times
    abide,
A land where Dakas and Dakinis assemble,
A land of which there is no higher,
Considering this, please remain in this land.

Please remain with your body like a vajra,
Please remain with your speech like a pure melody,
Please remain with your mind like the sun and the
    moon,

Please remain with your life like the king of mountains,
Please remain with your good qualities like an ocean,
Please remain with your deeds like the flow of a river.

O Losang, Principal Buddha, Vajradhara,
Please reveal your all-pervasive outer, inner, and secret
    bodies;
And with a compassionate intention towards migrators
    as extensive as space,
Please turn the outer, inner, and secret Dharma Wheels.

From the great play of the exalted mirror-like wisdom,
Please reveal the form of the all-pervasive Buddha
    lineage;
And with a compassionate intention towards migrators
    as extensive as space,
Please turn the outer, inner, and secret Dharma Wheels.

From the great play of the exalted wisdom of
    individual analysis,
Please reveal the form of the all-pervasive Päma
    lineage;
And with a compassionate intention towards migrators
    as extensive as space,
Please turn the outer, inner, and secret Dharma Wheels.

From the great play of the exalted wisdom of the
    Dharmadhatu,
Please reveal the form of the all-pervasive Vajra
    lineage;
And with a compassionate intention towards migrators
    as extensive as space,
Please turn the outer, inner, and secret Dharma Wheels.

From the great play of the exalted wisdom of equality,
Please reveal the form of the all-pervasive Ratna
    lineage;

And with a compassionate intention towards migrators
  as extensive as space,
Please turn the outer, inner, and secret Dharma Wheels.

From the great play of the exalted wisdom of
  accomplishing activities,
Please reveal the form of the all-pervasive Karma
  lineage;
And with a compassionate intention towards migrators
  as extensive as space,
Please turn the outer, inner, and secret Dharma Wheels.

Through requesting the supreme Dharma, the Principal
  Buddha and his retinue,
To turn the Wheel of Dharma for migrators,
May we have the fortune to accomplish the state of
  Losang Dorjechang
And then lead all migrators to that state.

Mandala offering requesting the Guru to remain

First the chant leader recites the following:

O Glorious and sacred Guru whose nature is inseparable
from the Great Conqueror, the all-pervasive Vajradhara,
Lord of an ocean of mandalas and lineages, endowed
with the meaning of the supreme symbols, incomparably
kind, great Spiritual Guide, Kelsang Gyatso Rinpoche,
may we offer in your presence a requesting mandala
beseeching you to remain with a life span of a hundred
thousand aeons for the sake of the doctrine and
migrators.

Now everyone recites:

OM VAJRA BHUMI AH HUM
Great and powerful golden ground,
OM VAJRA REKHE AH HUM
At the edge the iron fence stands around the outer
    circle.
In the centre, Mount Meru the king of mountains,
Around which are four continents:
In the east, Purvavideha, in the south, Jambudipa,
In the west, Aparagodaniya, in the north, Uttarakuru.
Each has two sub-continents:
Deha and Videha, Tsamara and Abatsamara,
Satha and Uttaramantrina, Kurava and Kaurava.
The mountain of jewels, the wish-granting tree,
The wish-granting cow, and the harvest unsown.
The precious wheel, the precious jewel,
The precious queen, the precious minister,
The precious elephant, the precious supreme horse,
The precious general, and the great treasure vase.
The goddess of beauty, the goddess of garlands,
The goddess of music, the goddess of dance,
The goddess of flowers, the goddess of incense,
The goddess of light, and the goddess of scent.
The sun and the moon, the precious umbrella,
The banner of victory in every direction.
In the centre all treasures of both gods and men,
An excellent collection with nothing left out.
We offer this to you, our kind root Guru and lineage
    Gurus,
And especially to you, Lord of an ocean of mandalas
    and lineages,
Endowed with the meaning of the supreme symbols,
Incomparably kind great Spiritual Guide, Kelsang
    Gyatso Rinpoche,

We offer in your presence a requesting mandala
beseeching you to remain with a life span of a
hundred thousand aeons for the sake of the doctrine
and migrators.
Please accept with compassion for migrating beings,
And having accepted, out of your great compassion,
Please bestow your blessings on all sentient beings
pervading space.

The ground sprinkled with perfume and spread with
flowers,
The Great Mountain, four lands, sun and moon,
Seen as a Buddha Land and offered thus,
May all beings enjoy such Pure Lands.

In the space before me on a lion throne, lotus, and
moon,
The venerable Gurus smile with delight.
O Supreme Field of Merit for our minds of faith,
Please remain for a hundred aeons to spread the
doctrine.

O Losang, Principal Buddha, Vajradhara,
Please reveal your all-pervasive outer, inner, and secret
bodies;
And with a compassionate intention towards migrators
as extensive as space,
Please turn the outer, inner, and secret Dharma Wheels.

*At this point the principal supplicant may deliver a praise
of the Guru's supreme qualities.*

IDAM GURU RATNA MANDALAKAM NIRYATAYAMI

Offering the representation of body

O Venerable Guru, embodiment of the Conquerors of
the three times,
Whose beautiful form is an inexhaustible treasury of
ornaments,
Please remain until samsara has ceased
As one whom to see, to hear, and to remember is so
meaningful.

Offering the representation of speech

O Venerable Guru, embodiment of the Conquerors of
the three times,
Whose melodious speech is an inexhaustible treasury
of ornaments,
Please bestow a feast of benefit and happiness on all
migrators
With your nectar of vast and profound Dharma.

Offering the representation of mind

O Venerable Guru, embodiment of the Conquerors of
the three times,
Whose secret mind is an inexhaustible treasury of
ornaments,
Please remain firm without ever moving from the
profound yogas
Of the six perfections and the two Tantric stages.

Offering the nam jar

O Glorious Guru, embodiment of all the Conquerors,
Through our offering to you this stainless nam jar,
May you remain firm like an unchangeable swastika
And always hold aloft the victory banner of Buddha's
doctrine.

Offering the chö gö

O Glorious Guru, embodiment of all the Conquerors,
Through our offering to you this stainless chö gö,
May you remain firm like an unchangeable swastika
And may the whole world be pervaded by pure moral
  discipline.

Offering the sham tab

O Glorious Guru, embodiment of all the Conquerors,
Through our offering to you this stainless sham tab,
May you remain firm like an unchangeable swastika
And may the explanation and practice of the three sets
  of doctrine increase.

Offering the Pandit's hat

O Glorious Guru, embodiment of all the Conquerors,
Through our offering to you this beautiful, yellow
  Pandit's hat,
May the lineage of pure view and pure deeds increase
And may the Ganden tradition spread throughout the
  ten directions.

Offering the ding wa

O Glorious Guru, embodiment of all the Conquerors,
Through our offering to you this ding wa, a fitting
  possession,
May you remain firm like an unchangeable swastika
And may unimpeded concentration spread throughout
  the ten directions.

Offering the bowl

O Glorious Guru, embodiment of all the Conquerors,
Through our offering to you this bowl brimming with
    food,
May your form remain firm like the king of mountains
And bestow a feast of vast and profound Dharma.

Offering the staff

O Glorious Guru, embodiment of all the Conquerors,
Through our offering to you this staff symbolizing the
    thirty-seven realizations of enlightenment,
May Losang Gyalwa's doctrines of scripture and
    realization
Always be held aloft by great beings with powerful
    hearts.

Offering the seven precious possessions of a king

Through our offering to you these seven precious
    possessions of a king,
Symbolic of the dominion over this world
Of the Mahayana Dharma praised by all the
    Conquerors of the three times,
May the reign of the King of Dharma last forever.

Offering the eight auspicious signs

We offer you these eight supremely auspicious signs:
A wheel, a victory banner, a parasol, a knot,
A lotus, an excellent vase, a golden fish, and a
    clockwise conch,
So that virtue and excellence may increase throughout
    all times and all directions.

Offering the mirror

The following is recited by the principal supplicant:

Just as a mirror was offered to the Blessed One, Buddha Shakyamuni, by Ö Changma, the Goddess of Form, and thereby became blessed as an auspicious substance; in the same way, on this occasion, in dependence upon the substance of this mirror, may the glorious sacred Guru, the great Spiritual Guide, the supreme Kelsang Gyatso Rinpoche, live for a hundred aeons.

Now the whole assembly recites:

May you remain.

This mirror is a vast ocean of exalted wisdom,
A supremely pure ocean of exalted wisdom.
May there be the auspiciousness of unobstructed
   enjoyment of completely pure Dharma
And may all obstructions be purified.

Offering the gi wang

The following is recited by the principal supplicant:

Just as gi wang was offered to the Blessed One, Buddha Shakyamuni, by Nor Kyong, the elephant, and thereby became blessed as an auspicious substance; in the same way, on this occasion, in dependence upon the substance of this gi wang, may the glorious sacred Guru, the great Spiritual Guide, the supreme Kelsang Gyatso Rinpoche, live for a hundred aeons.

Now the whole assembly recites:

May you remain.

This gi wang is medicine that destroys the sickness of
   the three poisons,
The supreme medicine of a complete realization of the
   nature of phenomena.
May there be the auspiciousness of the eradication of
   the pain of delusions
And may all suffering be purified.

Offering the curd

The following is recited by the principal supplicant:

Just as curd was offered to the Blessed One, Buddha
Shakyamuni, by Leg Kyema, the rural maiden, and
thereby became blessed as an auspicious substance; in
the same way, on this occasion, in dependence upon
the substance of this curd, may the glorious sacred
Guru, the great Spiritual Guide, the supreme Kelsang
Gyatso Rinpoche, live for a hundred aeons.

Now the whole assembly recites:

May you remain.

This curd is the essence of everything.
Having realized the essence that is the pure, supreme
   exalted wisdom,
May there be the auspiciousness of attaining the
   sphere of all qualities
And may the three poisons be pacified.

Offering the couch grass

The following is recited by the principal supplicant:

Just as couch grass was offered to the Blessed One,
Buddha Shakyamuni, by Trashi, the son of a grass-seller,

and thereby became blessed as an auspicious substance; in the same way, on this occasion, in dependence upon the substance of this couch grass, may the glorious sacred Guru, the great Spiritual Guide, the supreme Kelsang Gyatso Rinpoche, live for a hundred aeons.

Now the whole assembly recites:

May you remain.

This couch grass increases lifespan.
Having accomplished the lifespan of Vajrasattva,
May there be the auspiciousness of the cessation of
    deluded life and death
And may lifespan be increased.

Offering the precious fruit

The following is recited by the principal supplicant:

Just as precious fruit was offered to the Blessed One, Buddha Shakyamuni, by Brahma, and thereby became blessed as an auspicious substance; in the same way, on this occasion, in dependence upon the substance of this precious fruit, may the glorious sacred Guru, the great Spiritual Guide, the supreme Kelsang Gyatso Rinpoche, live for a hundred aeons.

Now the whole assembly recites:

May you remain.

This precious fruit is the Dharma of causes, conditions,
    and their results –
All mundane and supramundane deeds.
May there be the auspiciousness of the supremely pure
    essence of enlightenment
And may all purposes be accomplished.

Offering the conch

The following is recited by the principal supplicant:

Just as a conch was offered to the Blessed One, Buddha Shakyamuni, by Indra, the king of the gods, and thereby became blessed as an auspicious substance; in the same way, on this occasion, in dependence upon the substance of this conch, may the glorious sacred Guru, the great Spiritual Guide, the supreme Kelsang Gyatso Rinpoche, live for a hundred aeons.

Now while a conch is blown, the whole assembly recites:

May you remain.

This conch, the means for proclaiming the sound of
    Dharma,
Is the pure essence of an ocean of exalted wisdom.
May there be the auspiciousness of the unmistaken
    Dharma being completely revealed
And may words be endowed with power.

Offering the sindhura

The following is recited by the principal supplicant:

Just as sindhura was offered to the Blessed One, Buddha Shakyamuni, by the King of the Brahmins, and thereby became blessed as an auspicious substance; in the same way, on this occasion, in dependence upon the substance of this sindhura, may the glorious sacred Guru, the great Spiritual Guide, the supreme Kelsang Gyatso Rinpoche, live for a hundred aeons.

Now the whole assembly recites:

May you remain.

This red sindhura is the nature of power,
The powerful condensation of all unmistaken Dharma.
May there be the auspiciousness of the rule of Dharma
    remaining forever
And may you always reign firm.

Offering the white mustard seed

The following is recited by the principal supplicant:

Just as the substance of white mustard seed,
accomplished by the Lord of Secret Mantra and
Knowledge Mantras, Vajrapani, was offered to the
Blessed One, Buddha Shakyamuni, and thereby
became blessed as an auspicious substance; in the
same way, on this occasion, in dependence upon the
substance of this white mustard seed, may the glorious
sacred Guru, the great Spiritual Guide, the supreme
Kelsang Gyatso Rinpoche, live for a hundred aeons.

Now the whole assembly recites:

May you remain.

This white mustard seed is all the vajra lineages,
With the power, good qualities, and excellence
To overcome all obstacles.
May there be this auspiciousness, and may all
    obstructions be pacified.

*At this point the whole assembly offers scarves and other
offerings to the Guru while reciting his long life prayers.*

Spontaneous Accomplishment of Wishes

OM SÖTI

O Protector of the Land of Bliss who bestow without
  effort
The immeasurable joy of immortality the moment we
  think of your breathtaking body,
Beautified by the major and minor marks,
Please send down a rain of attainments of long life
  and exalted wisdom.

You who are skilled in the wisdom that unties the
  sealed knots
Of the profound meaning of the Sutras and Tantras of
  the Fourth Deliverer of this fortunate aeon,
Who possess an abundance of good qualities like a
  thousand-petalled lotus,
O Peerless, great Spiritual Guide, may you live for a
  very long time.

The holy Dharma, a treasury of jewels that is difficult
  to find for many aeons,
Is borne forth on the chariot of your excellent, superior
  intention;
O Protector who destroy the samsaric miseries of vast
  numbers of disciples,
Great Knowledge Hero arisen from an ocean (of wisdom),
  may you live for a very long time.

Through the stream of nectar of your eloquent
  instructions
Ripening well at the essence of our hearts,
And bringing to maturity the bodily strength of the
  Mahayana paths,
May we be able to fulfil the hopes of countless
  migrators.

Through the force of the three secrets of the Conquerors
and their Sons,
The virtuous deeds of the powerful, oath-bound
Protectors,
And the dependent-arising of the faith and respect of
myself and other disciples,
May our prayers be accomplished according to our
wishes.

A Heavenly Song of Immortality Requesting the Guru to Remain Forever

HRIH

Refuge and Protector of all migrators, including the
gods,
Matchless, venerable Spiritual Guide, closest friend
and helper,
Whose nature is the three lineages of Losang Dragpa,
O Sublime lamp illuminating the three worlds, to you
we offer praise.

Supreme Spiritual Guide who arose from the magical
sphere of compassion,
To reveal to migrators like us who have little fortune
The path to liberation of the fortunate ones;
O What great good fortune to have met you!

We request all the Long-life Deities abiding in the
supreme places such as Sukhavati,
Resplendent with a thousand light rays of the major
and minor marks,
To send down an inexhaustible stream of the nectar
of immortality
To prolong the life of the glorious Spiritual Guide.

In these impure times you manifest forms
According to the fortunes of each disciple;
You are endowed with the excellence of learning and
    purity;
O Supreme ocean of infinite good qualities, to you we
    make requests.

The doctrine of Buddha, and especially the doctrine of
    Protector Manjushri's whispered lineage,
Exist through the kindness of the previous holy beings,
Now you reveal this excellent, unmistaken path to
    fortunate disciples;
O Spiritual Guide, we request you to remain.

In these degenerate times you cherish the Buddhadharma,
You show living beings the path to freedom and
    happiness,
And you possess a great wealth of honesty, scholarship,
    and renown;
And yet because these times are so impure we are unable
    to repay your kindness; O Please be patient with us.

Through the profound intention that you previously
    generated,
And remembering the kindness of your own Spiritual
    Guide,
May you remain for a very long time, always performing
    your excellent deeds,
Taking on the great responsibility of caring in every
    way for the doctrine and migrators.

O Protector please remain firm for countless aeons
With the nature of an indestructible vajra
So that all directions will be pervaded by your
    matchless, excellent deeds
Of spreading this excellent, stainless tradition.

Through the blessings of the Guru and Three Precious
   Jewels,
The sublime assistance of the Yidams and Dharma
   Protectors,
And our faithful, heartfelt requests,
May all wishes be accomplished.

Especially through the force of the blessings of the
   Vajra Queen
And the virtuous deeds of the Great Vajra King,
May the venerable Spiritual Guide Kelsang Gyatso
   have a very long life,
And may all his activities flourish.

Throughout all our lives may the supreme, venerable
   Guru
Gladly take us all into his loving care;
And without ever being parted from him may we
   complete the grounds and paths,
And accomplish bodies endowed with all the qualities
   of abandonment and realization.

Thanking mandala

First the chant leader recites the following:

O Glorious and sacred Guru whose nature is inseparable
from the Great Conqueror, the all-pervasive Vajradhara,
Lord of an ocean of mandalas and lineages, endowed
with the meaning of the supreme symbols, incomparably
kind, great Spiritual Guide, Kelsang Gyatso Rinpoche,
may we offer in your presence a thanking mandala
thanking you for your kindness in perfectly and
profoundly accepting our request to remain with a
life span of a hundred thousand aeons for the sake
of the doctrine and migrators.

Now everyone recites:

OM VAJRA BHUMI AH HUM
Great and powerful golden ground,
OM VAJRA REKHE AH HUM
At the edge the iron fence stands around the outer
   circle.
In the centre, Mount Meru the king of mountains,
Around which are four continents:
In the east, Purvavideha, in the south, Jambudipa,
In the west, Aparagodaniya, in the north, Uttarakuru.
Each has two sub-continents:
Deha and Videha, Tsamara and Abatsamara,
Satha and Uttaramantrina, Kurava and Kaurava.
The mountain of jewels, the wish-granting tree,
The wish-granting cow, and the harvest unsown.
The precious wheel, the precious jewel,
The precious queen, the precious minister,
The precious elephant, the precious supreme horse,
The precious general, and the great treasure vase.
The goddess of beauty, the goddess of garlands,
The goddess of music, the goddess of dance,
The goddess of flowers, the goddess of incense,
The goddess of light, and the goddess of scent.
The sun and the moon, the precious umbrella,
The banner of victory in every direction.
In the centre all treasures of both gods and men,
An excellent collection with nothing left out.
We offer this to you, our kind root Guru and lineage
   Gurus,
And especially to you, Lord of an ocean of mandalas
   and lineages,
Endowed with the meaning of the supreme symbols,
Incomparably kind great Spiritual Guide, Kelsang
   Gyatso Rinpoche,

We offer in your presence a thanking mandala
  thanking you for your kindness in perfectly and
  profoundly accepting our request to remain with a
  life span of a hundred thousand aeons for the sake
  of the doctrine and migrators.
Please accept with compassion for migrating beings,
And having accepted, out of your great compassion,
Please bestow your blessings on all sentient beings
  pervading space.

The ground sprinkled with perfume and spread with
  flowers,
The Great Mountain, four lands, sun and moon,
Seen as a Buddha Land and offered thus,
May all beings enjoy such Pure Lands.

From the billowing clouds of wisdom and compassion
In the space of your Truth Body, O Venerable and holy
  Gurus,
Please send down a rain of vast and profound Dharma
Appropriate to the disciples of this world.

May the life span of the Venerable Guru remain firm,
May his pure, virtuous deeds spread throughout the
  ten directions,
And may the lamp of Losang Dragpa's doctrine
  always shine
Dispelling the ignorance of migrators throughout the
  three worlds.

IDAM GURU RATNA MANDALAKAM NIRYATAYAMI

Tea and rice are now served.

Praise and Request to Buddha Amitayus

O Protector Amitayus, born from a HRIH,
On a moon seat upon a thousand-petalled lotus,
With a vermilion colour like the young rising sun
Covered with a pleasing, red-yellow veil.

I prostrate to you whose body is completely beautified
By various garments and many jewelled ornaments,
Like a ruby mountain
Completely covered by the rays of the sun.

I prostrate to you who grant the attainment of life
From a bowl brimming with the nectar of immortality
That you hold in the centre of your two hands,
As supple as the branches of a young sapling.

I prostrate to you ablaze with the brilliant splendour
    of the signs and indications,
Whose crown is adorned with a top-knot, black as jet,
From which there hangs a long plait;
And who wear a lower garment of various fine,
    smooth silks.

I prostrate to you who bestow all goodness,
And with my palms pressed together out of very
    strong faith
I proclaim well your excellent qualities
With a sweet-sounding voice that captures the heart.

I prostrate to you who are a lasting source of refuge,
Whose sword of wisdom cuts the net of unknowing,
Whose compassion for all living beings is without
    interruption,
And who tirelessly assume the burden of liberating all
    migrators.

I prostrate to you for all time.
Just by calling your name, untimely death is destroyed;
By mentally recalling you, we are protected from the
    fears of samsara and peace;
And by relying upon you as a refuge, a lasting
    happiness is conferred.

With devotion I rely upon you who are free from faults.
Temporarily, may all undesired dangers be pacified,
And ultimately may I be spontaneously born from a
    lotus
In Blissful Land and do what pleases you.

Now Offering to the Spiritual Guide *is resumed with
the verse requesting the Spiritual Guide not to pass away.*

*The tsog offering for the spirits is taken out at the usual
point, after which the* Song of the Spring Queen *is
recited. The verse gathering and dissolving the Field of
Merit is not recited on this occasion.*

Colophon: These prayers were compiled from traditional
sources by Venerable Chöyang Duldzin Kuten for the
faithful disciples of Geshe Kelsang Gyatso Rinpoche,
the students of the New Kadampa Tradition, in July 1988.